FLAT SKETCHING
FOR THE FASHION INDUSTRY

BY BARBARA SULTAN

Born in New York City. Barbara Sultan
has extensive experience as a clothing
designer.

A strong creative vision along with a
commitment to detail and quality have
been hallmarks to Sultan's 20 year career
as a fashion designer both in New York
and Los Angeles.

Sultan has been a teacher at the Fashion
Institute of Design and Merchandising in
Los Angeles for 19 years, where she currently
teaches drawing in the design, manufacturing
and product development programs. Sultan
lectures at various universities on design, art,
and the computer.

9TH PRINTING

Other books by Sultan:
Applied Flat Sketching for the Fashion Industry
Computer Aided Flat Sketching for the Fashion Industry

Library of Congress
catalog number TX 4-031-493

Copyright©1995 by Barbara Sultan
ISBN: 0-9647196-9-x

Published by :
DA-MAX
PO BOX 50575
LOS ANGELES CA 90050
WWW. DA-MAX.COM

printed in the USA

INTRODUCTION

The purpose of this book is to explain and demonstrate the technique of drawing a flat garment. It is a response to the need for a practical, comprehensive set of instructions for flat sketching.

In the fashion business, it is important to communicate your designs with a working sketch. This book has been designed so that the novice, as well as the professional, may accomplish this goal. The croquis illustrated in this book will provide a guide for accurate drawing. By carefully following each lesson, you will develop the skill of drawing a flat sketch with accurate proportions and details, and will be able to communicate an idea to all in the fashion industry.

The book may be used as a method of self instruction, a textbook, or a handy reference guide for industry professionals.   Your knowledge, skills, and confidence will increase as you practice each exercise.

TABLE OF CONTENTS

Use tracing paper over the croquis throughout the book to master the technique of flat sketching. Practice tracing each group of garments several times to develop speed and accuracy. As your skills increase, you will add your own details and style lines. All you need for this is pencils and tracing paper.

Terms

Croquis - A guide figure to trace over; a draft sketch

Centre Front (C.F.) - Centre of figure

B.Z. - Back zipper

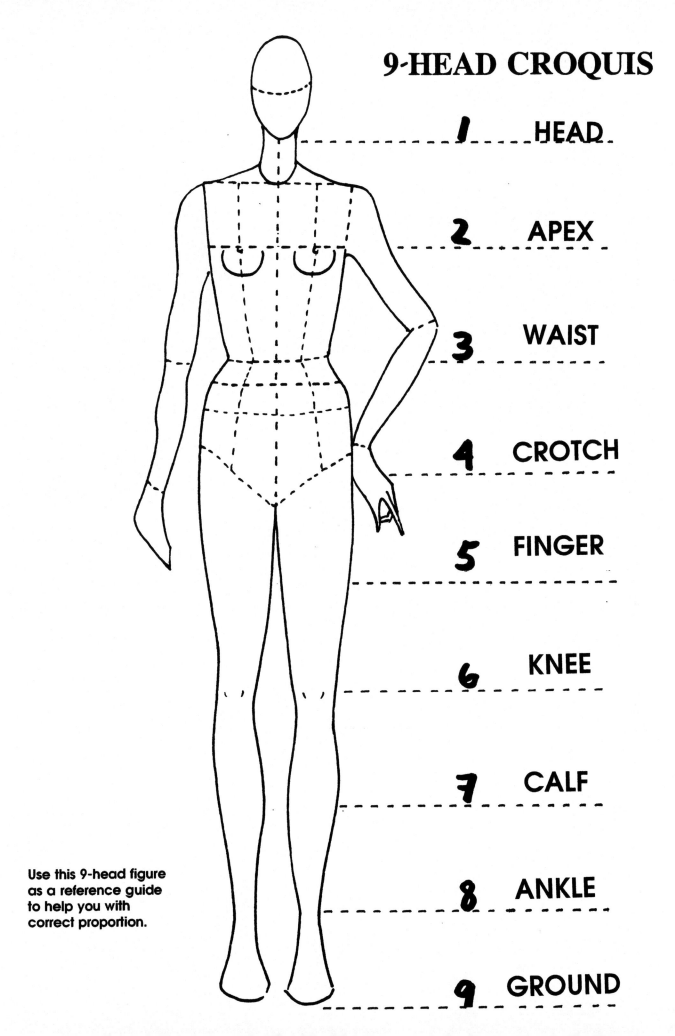

9-HEAD CROQUIS

1 — HEAD

2 — APEX

3 — WAIST

4 — CROTCH

5 — FINGER

6 — KNEE

7 — CALF

8 — ANKLE

9 — GROUND

Use this 9-head figure as a reference guide to help you with correct proportion.

1

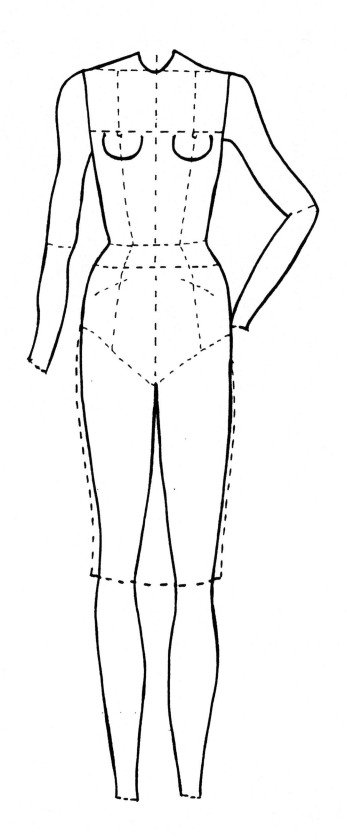

NOTE :

FOR SKIRT
PLACEMENT

LINE UP
TRACING PAPER
ON CROQUIS

FIND
CENTRE FRONT

FITTED
SKIRT

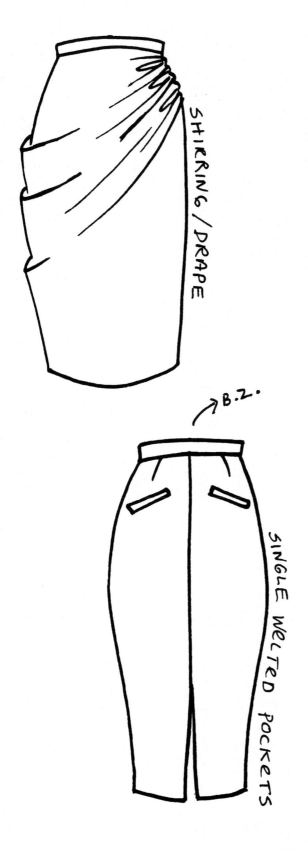

SHIRRING / DRAPE

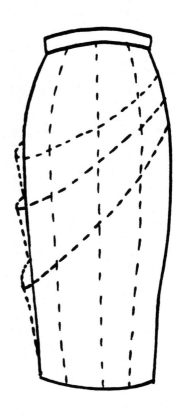

B.Z.

SINGLE WELTED POCKETS

BELT LOOPS ←

→fly front
placement

Taper evenly to
hemline

**Develop the A-line
skirt design by tracing
on the croquis. Use
different hemlines,
seamlines and
waistbands.**

4

A-LINE SKIRT

B.Z.

A-LINE / w/ YOKE

5

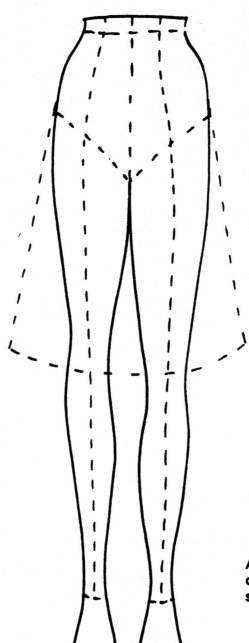

After tracing skirt, draw
a new style using the same
silhouette.

GORE SKIRT

B.Z.

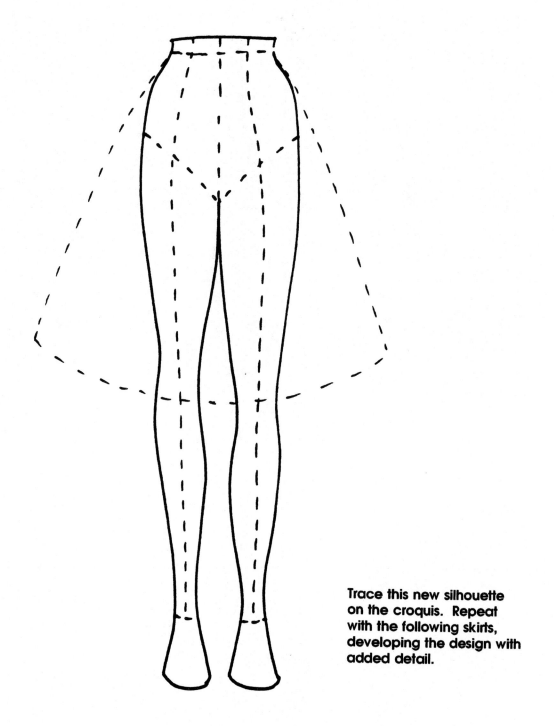

Trace this new silhouette
on the croquis. Repeat
with the following skirts,
developing the design with
added detail.

GATHERED
SKIRT

3-TIER / ELASTIC WAISTBAND

9

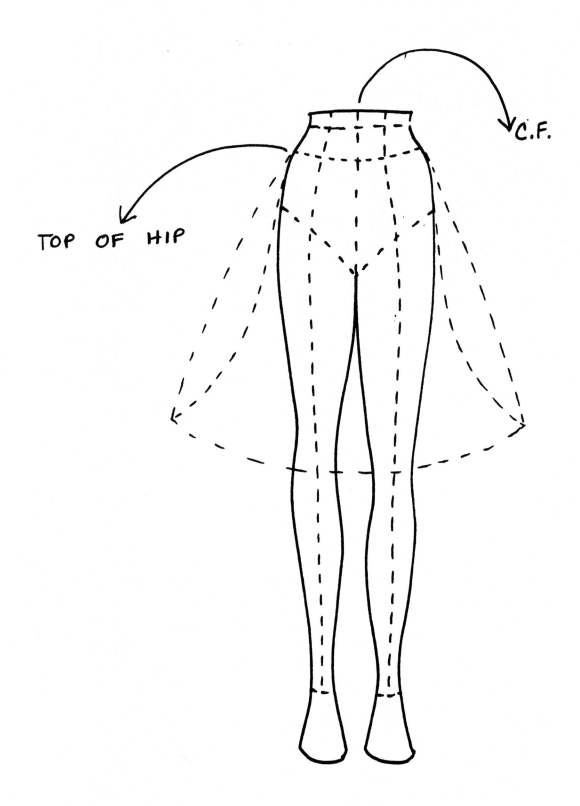

TOP OF HIP

C.F.

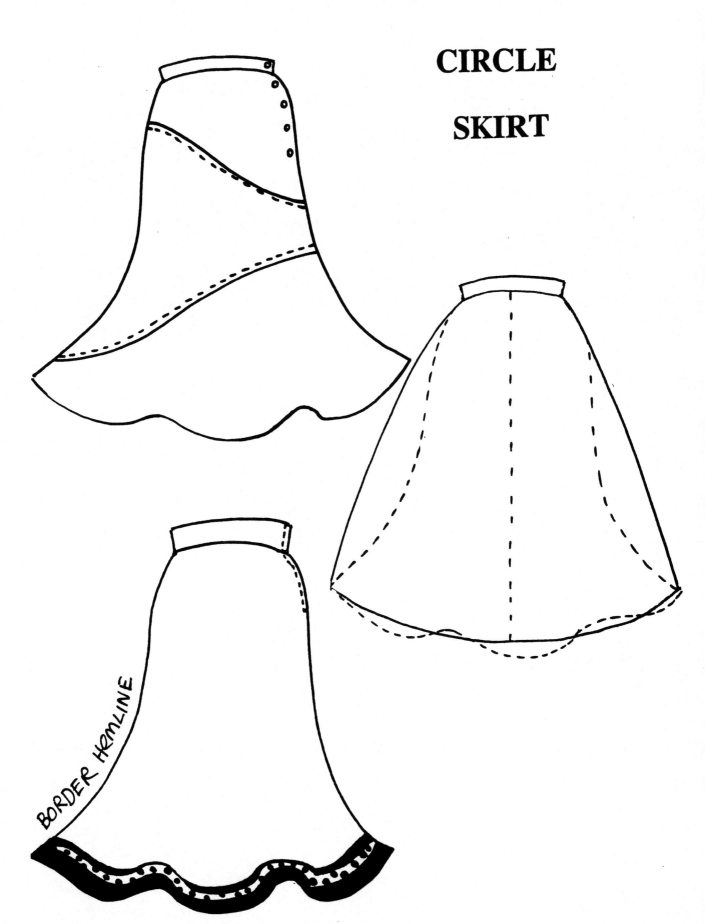

CIRCLE

SKIRT

BORDER HEMLINE

11

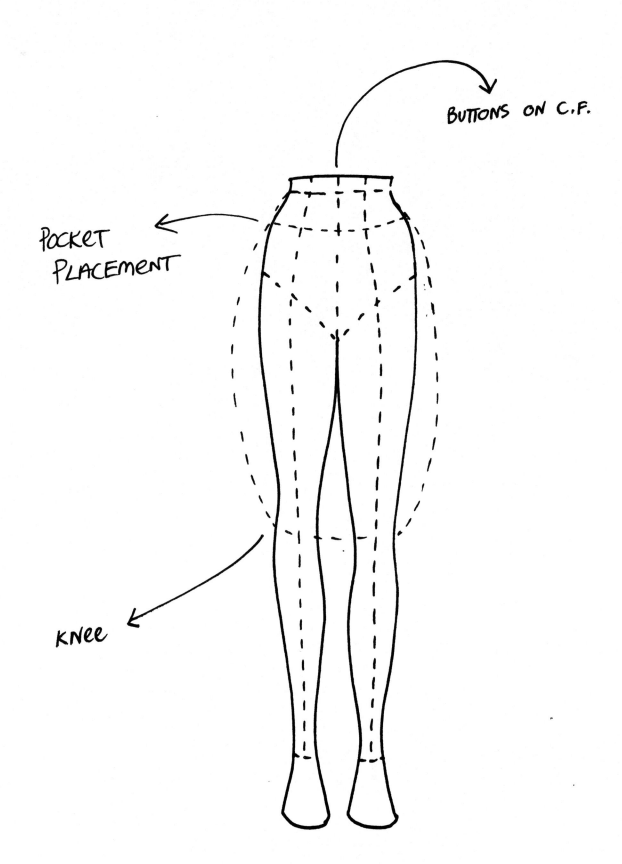

BUTTONS ON C.F.

POCKET PLACEMENT

KNEE

BUBBLE SKIRT

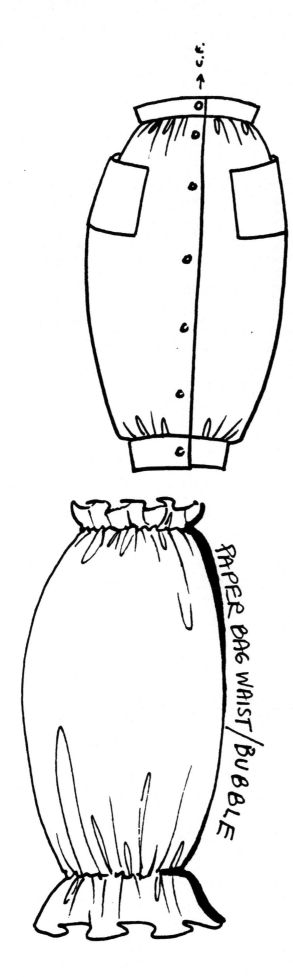

PAPER BAG WAIST/BUBBLE

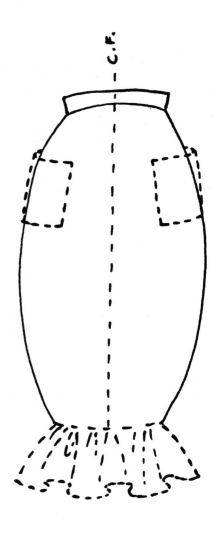

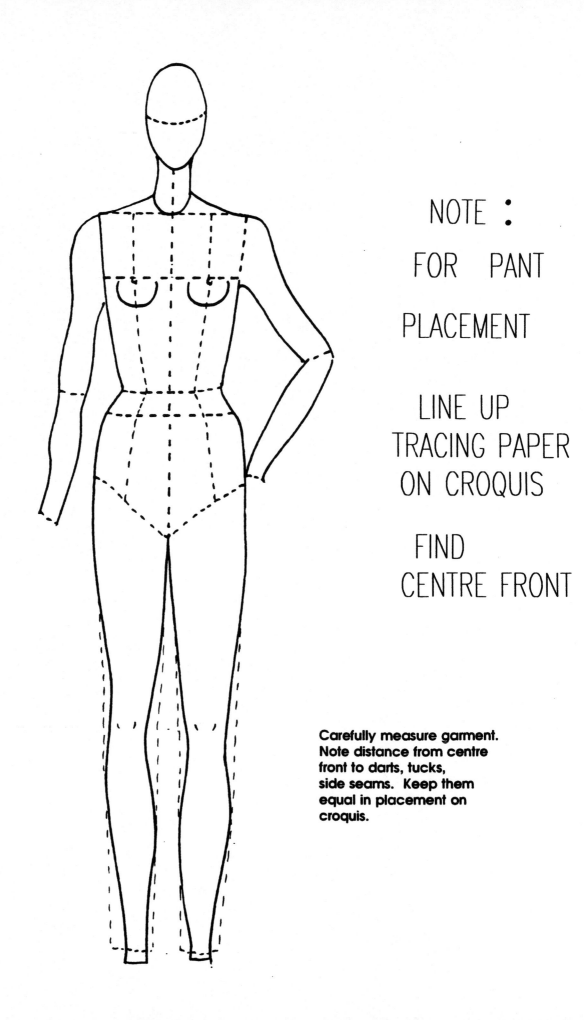

NOTE :
FOR PANT
PLACEMENT

LINE UP
TRACING PAPER
ON CROQUIS

FIND
CENTRE FRONT

Carefully measure garment.
Note distance from centre
front to darts, tucks,
side seams. Keep them
equal in placement on
croquis.

FITTED PANT

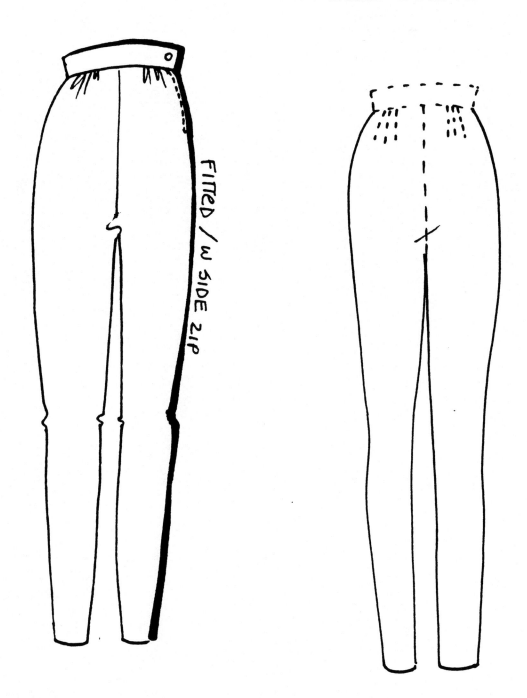

FITTED / w SIDE ZIP

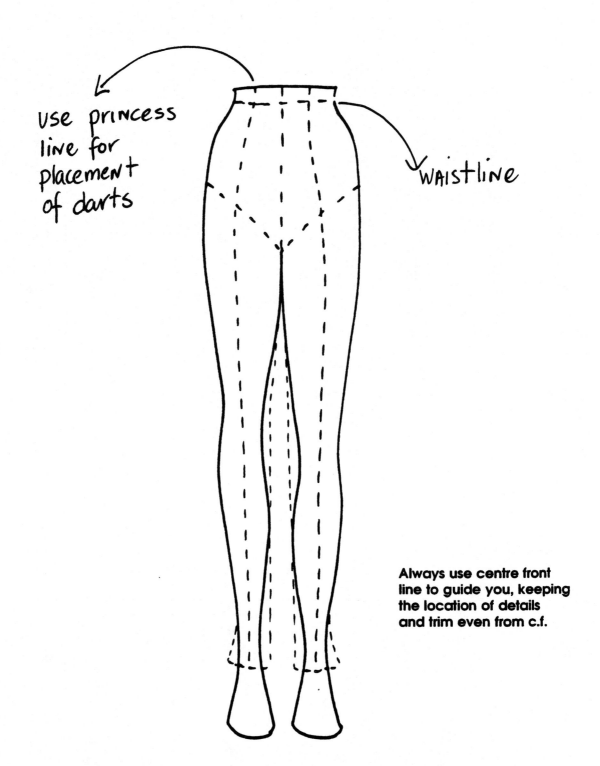

use princess line for placement of darts

waistline

Always use centre front line to guide you, keeping the location of details and trim even from c.f.

HIGH WAISTED PANT

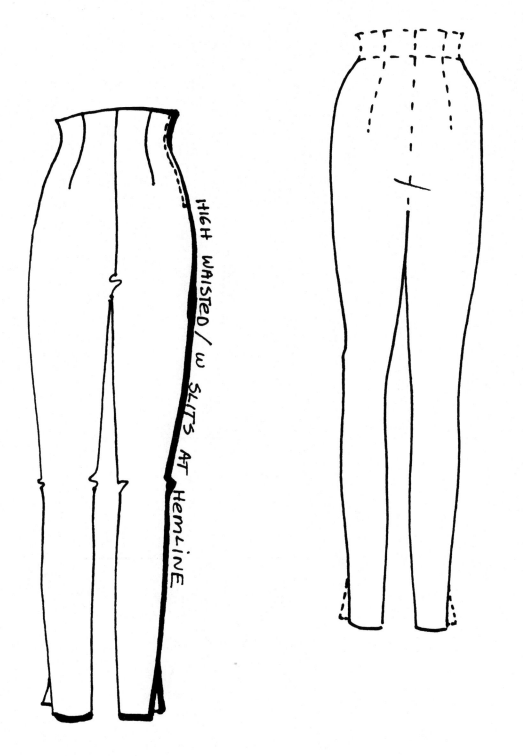

HIGH WAISTED / W SLITS AT HEMLINE

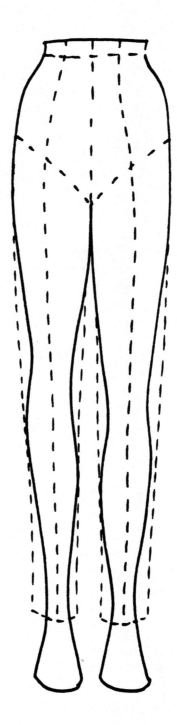

Practice drawing five
versions of this garment.

Repeat this process for
the following pants and
shorts.

JEANS

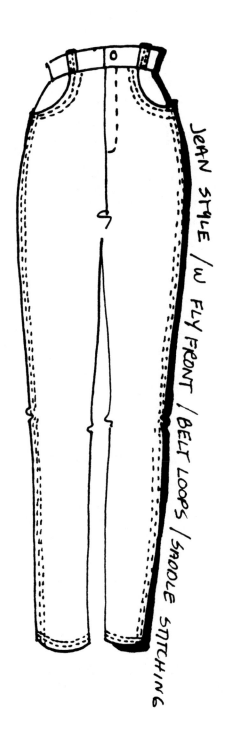

JEAN STYLE /W FLY FRONT / BELT LOOPS / SADDLE STITCHING

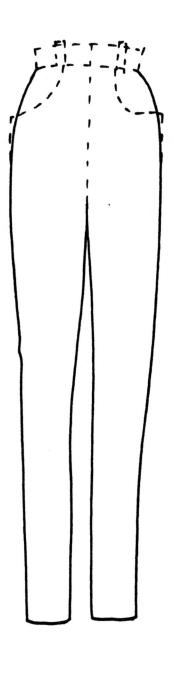

19

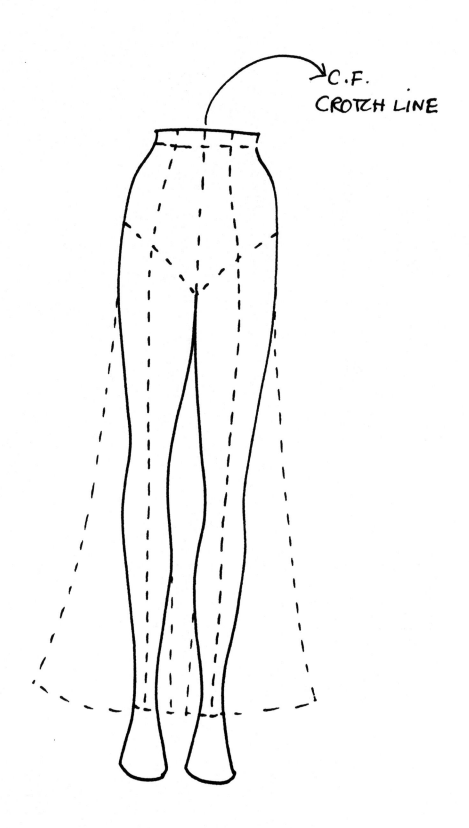

C.F.
CROTCH LINE

FULL PANT W/ ELASTIC

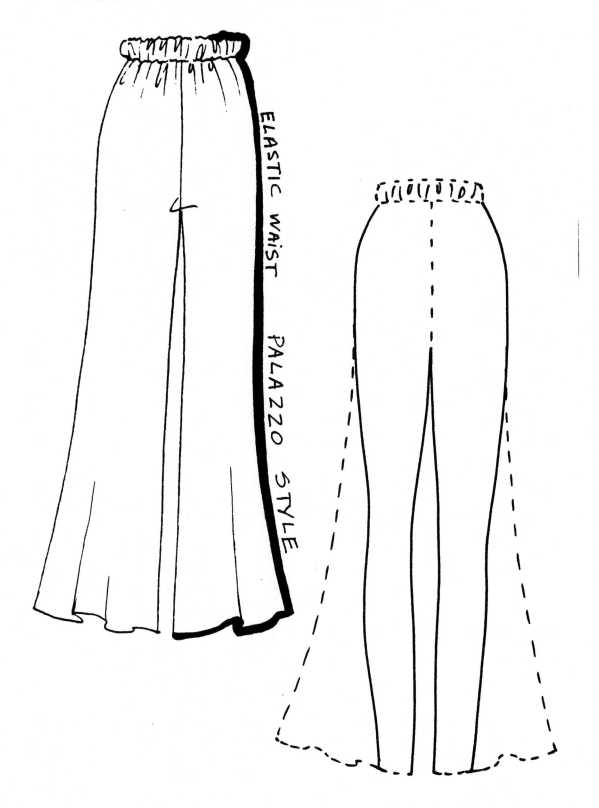

ELASTIC WAIST   PALAZZO STYLE

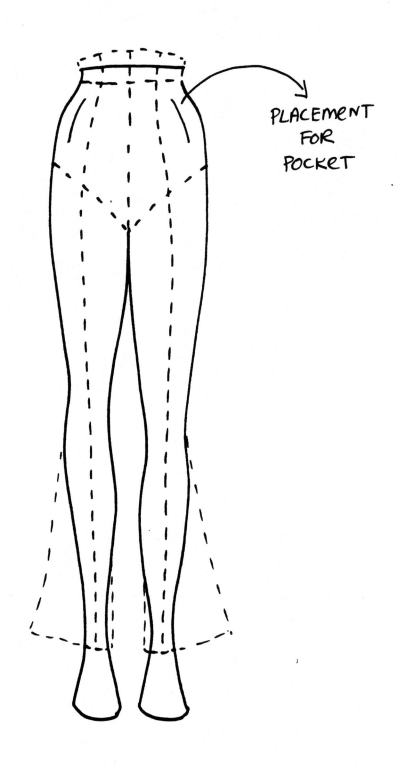

PLACEMENT
FOR
POCKET

BELL BOTTOMS

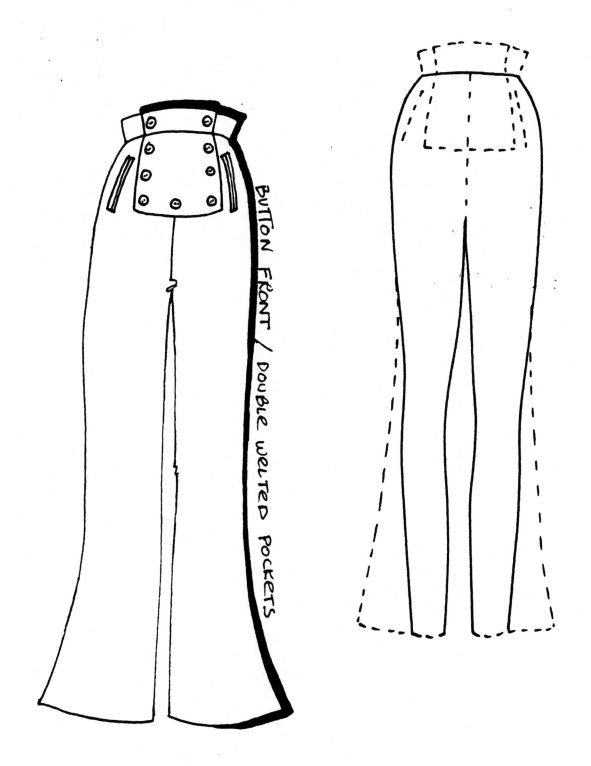

BUTTON FRONT / DOUBLE WELTED POCKETS

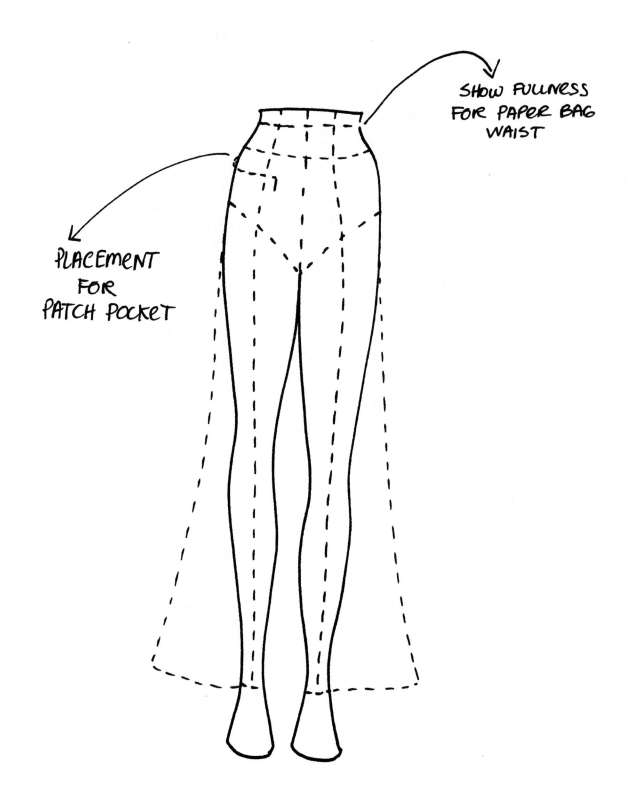

SHOW FULLNESS
FOR PAPER BAG
WAIST

PLACEMENT
FOR
PATCH POCKET

FULL PANT W/PAPER BAG WAIST

PAPER BAG WAIST / PATCH POCKETS

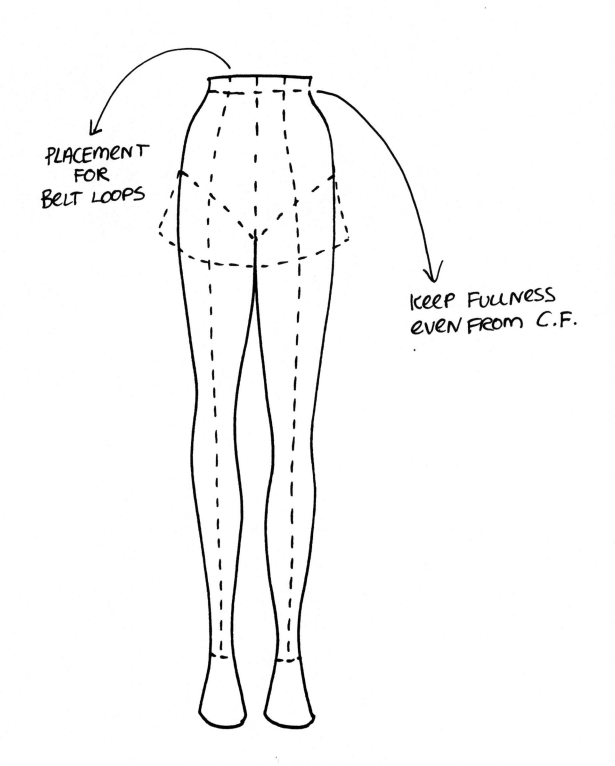

PLACEMENT
FOR
BELT LOOPS

KEEP FULLNESS
EVEN FROM C.F.

SHORTS

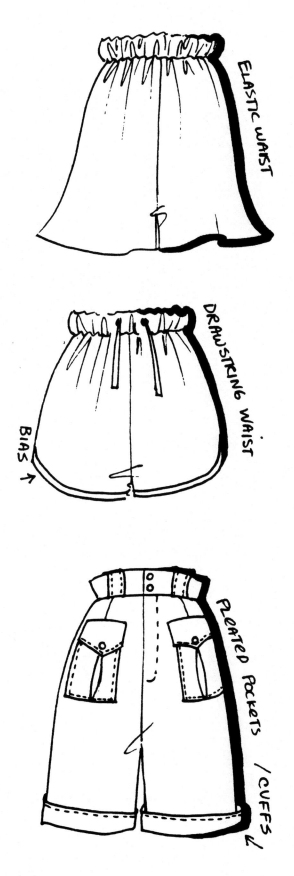

ELASTIC WAIST

DRAWSTRING WAIST

BIAS

PLEATED POCKETS / CUFFS

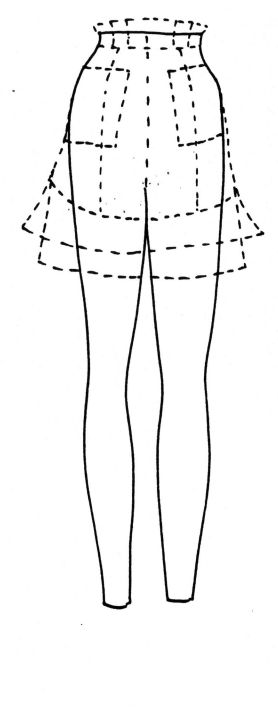

27

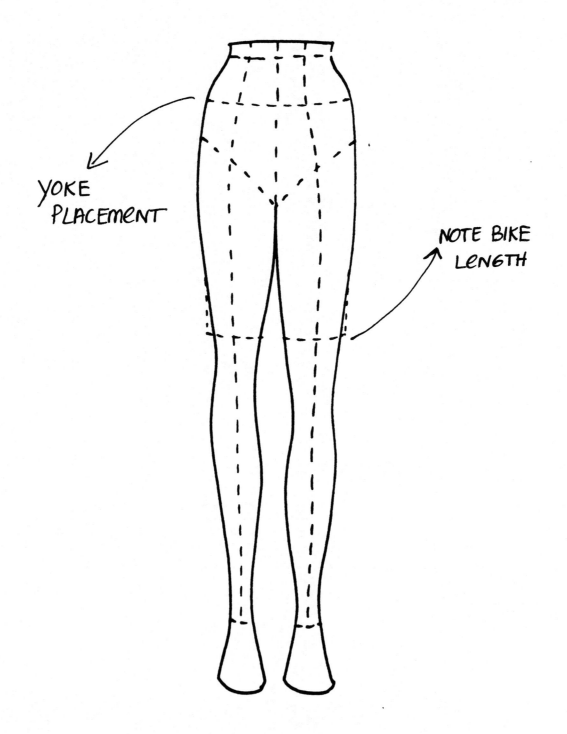

YOKE
PLACEMENT

NOTE BIKE
LENGTH

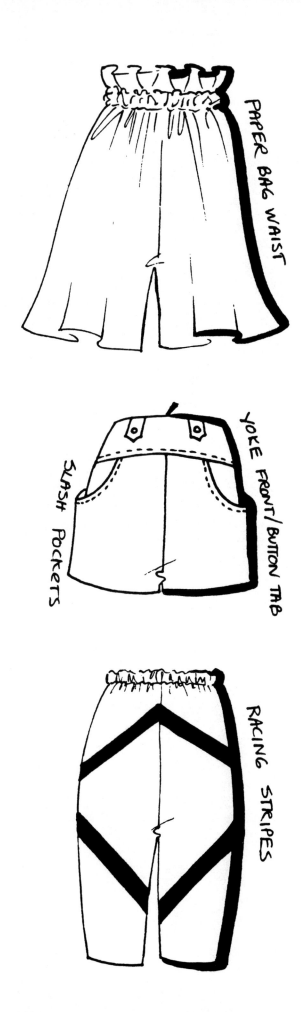

PAPER BAG WAIST

SLASH POCKETS

YOKE FRONT / BUTTON TAB

RACING STRIPES

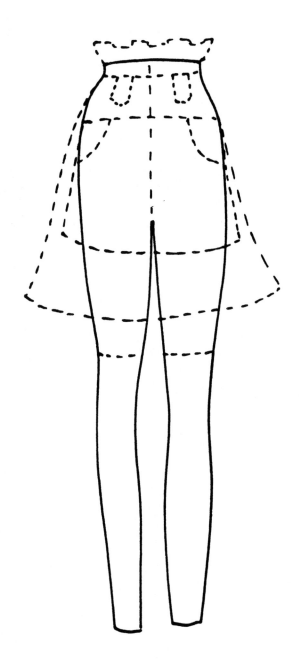

29

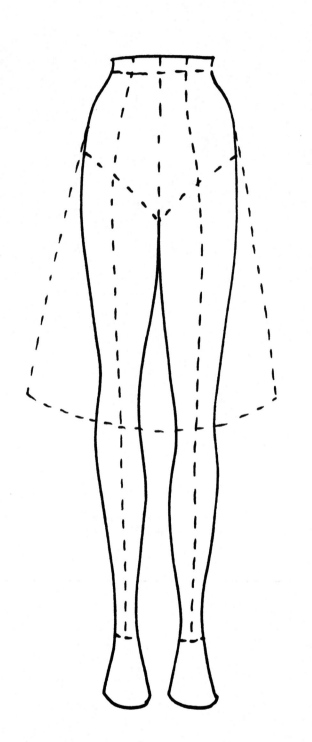

NOTE:
FOR

PLACEMENT

LINE UP
TRACING PAPER
ON CROQUIS

FIND
CENTRE FRONT

KNIFE PLEAT

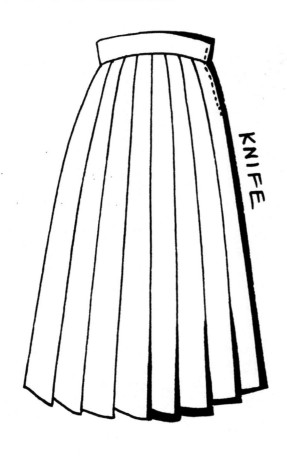

KNIFE

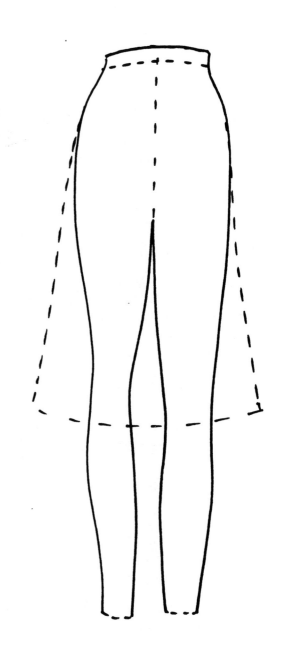

NOTE :

KNIFE PLEATS

FABRIC FOLDED
TO ONE SIDE.

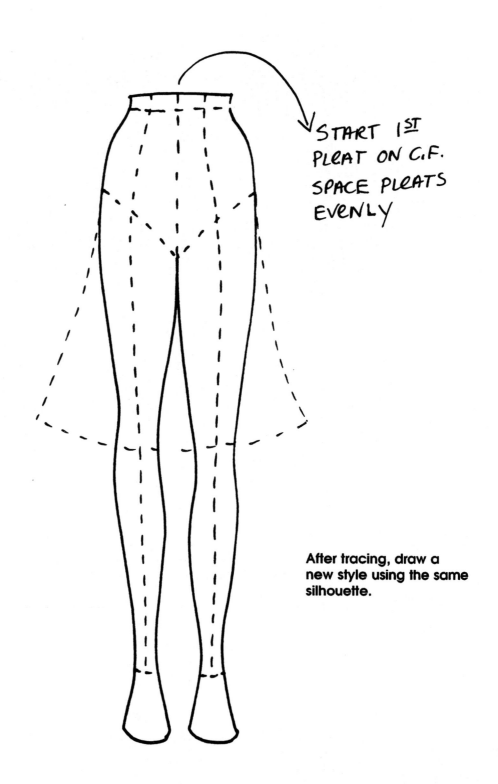

START 1ST
PLEAT ON C.F.
SPACE PLEATS
EVENLY

After tracing, draw a
new style using the same
silhouette.

ACCORDION PLEAT

ACCORDION

CRYSTAL PLEAT

CRYSTAL

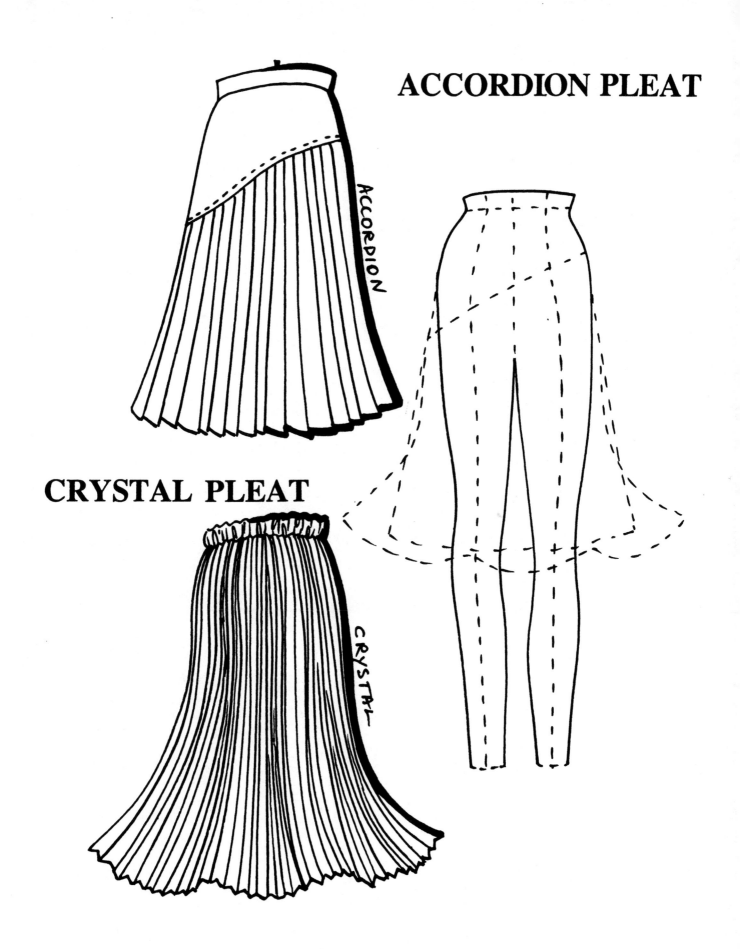

33

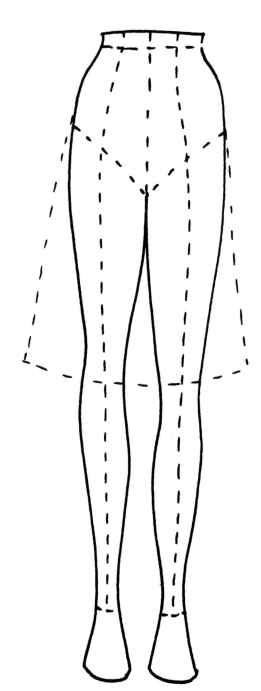

Continue to develop the new skirt design on the croquis. Use different hemlines, pocket treatments, seamlines, and waistbands.

BOX PLEAT

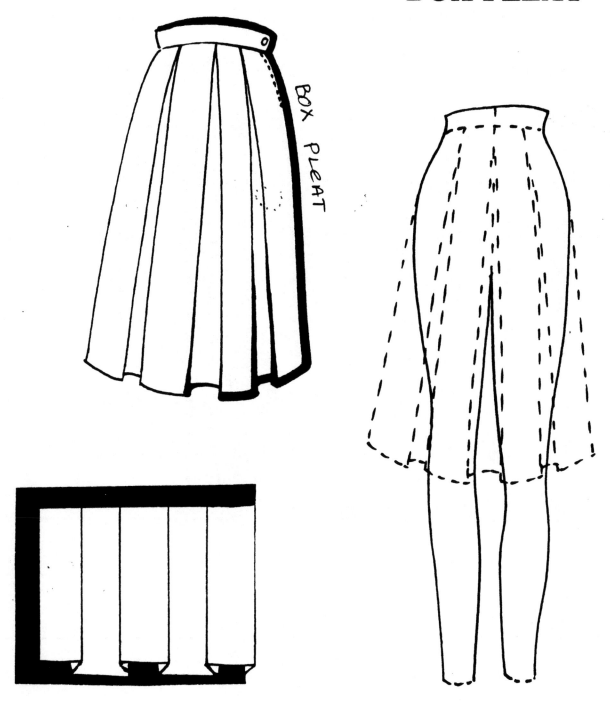

BOX PLEAT

BOX PLEATS

NOTE :   TWO KNIFE PLEATS
FACING EACH OTHER

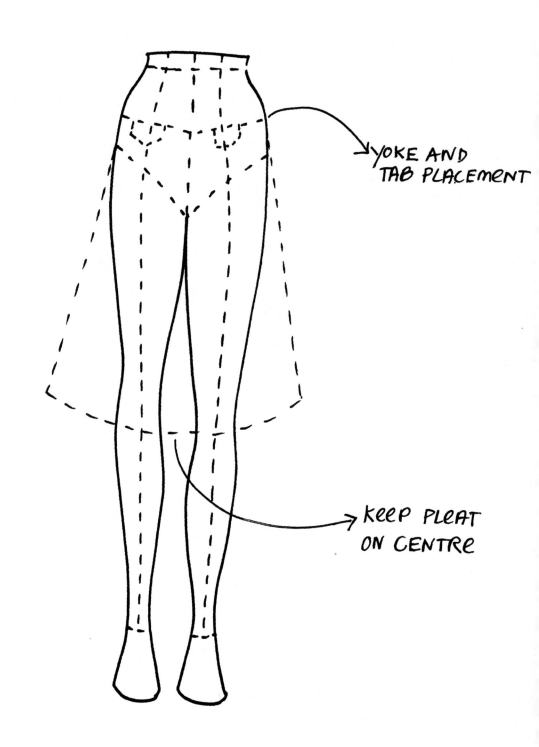

YOKE AND
TAB PLACEMENT

KEEP PLEAT
ON CENTRE

INVERTED

PLEAT

YOKE FRONT / INVERTED PLEAT

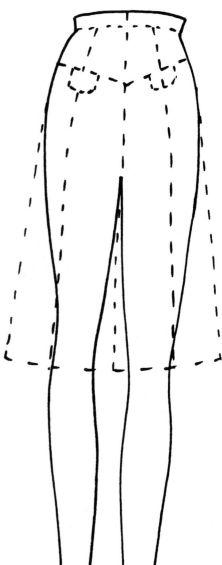

INVERTED
TWO FOLDS
FACING CENTRE

37

FOR SLEEVE PLACE-
MENT, LINE UP
TRACING PAPER
ON TOP OF CROQUIS.
FIND APEX AND
CENTRE FRONT.
NOTE DROP OF ARM-
HOLE FOR DIFFERENT
SLEEVES.

1. SET-IN SLEEVE
2. DROP SLEEVE
3. PUFF SLEEVE
4. RAGLAN SLEEVE
5. DOLMAN SLEEVE

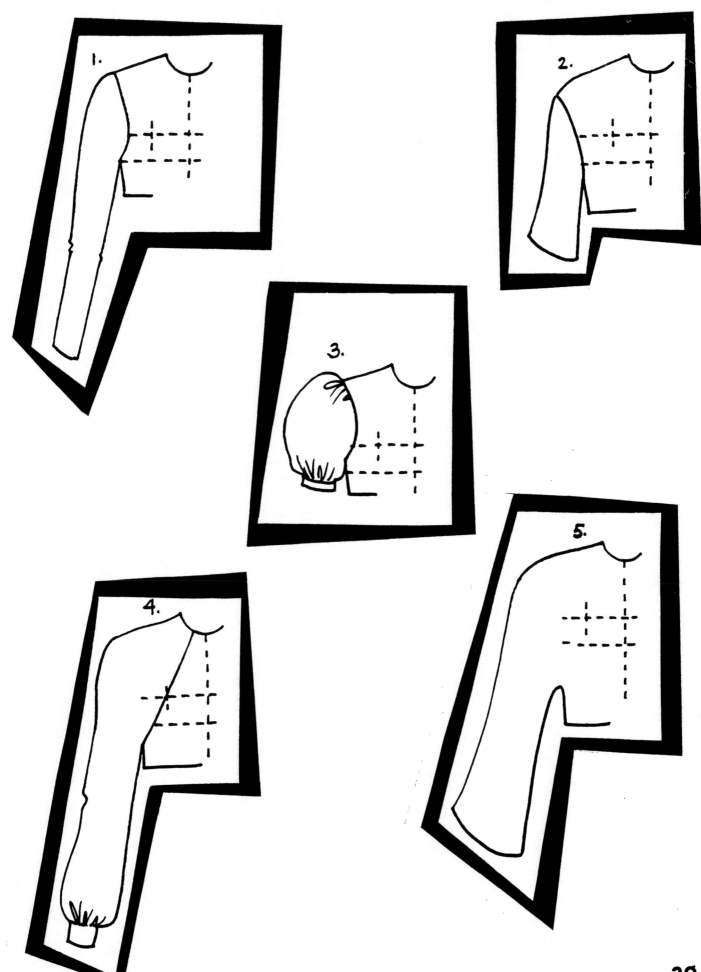

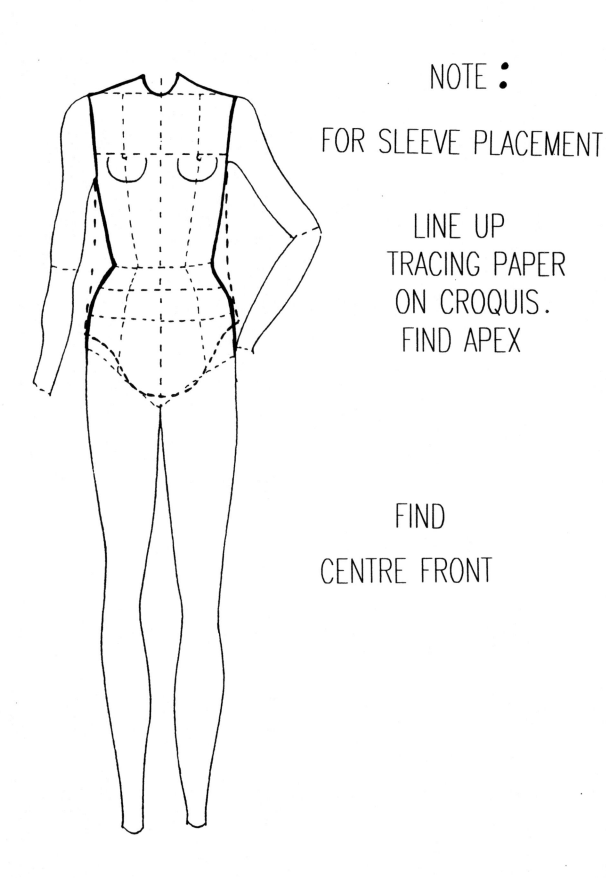

NOTE :

FOR SLEEVE PLACEMENT

LINE UP
TRACING PAPER
ON CROQUIS.
FIND APEX

FIND

CENTRE FRONT

BLOUSES

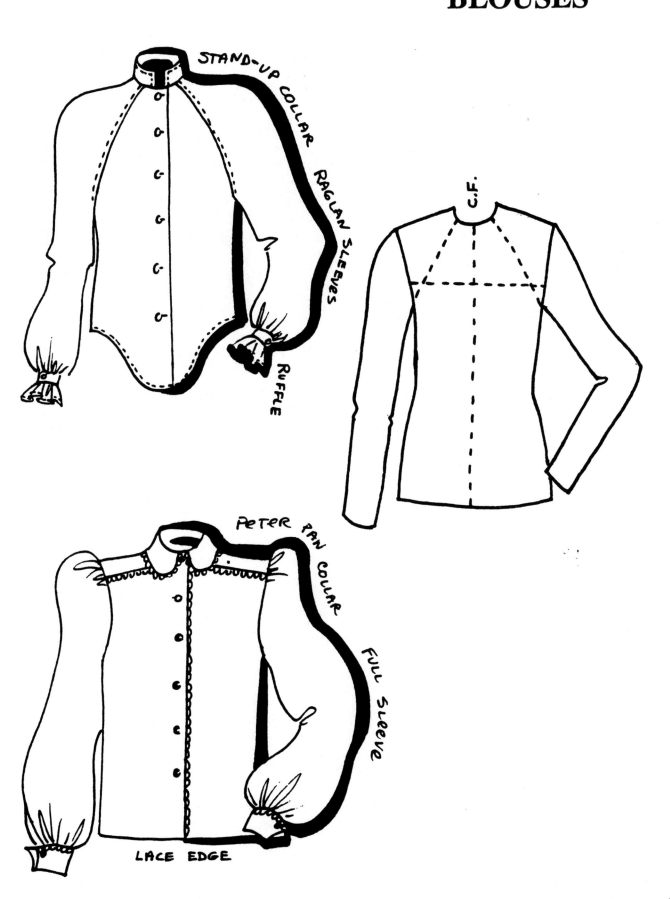

STAND-UP COLLAR

RAGLAN SLEEVES

RUFFLE

C.F.

PETER PAN COLLAR

FULL SLEEVE

LACE EDGE

DROP ARMHOLE
FOR SLEEVE

**Carefully measure garment.
Note distance from centre
front .**

TOP

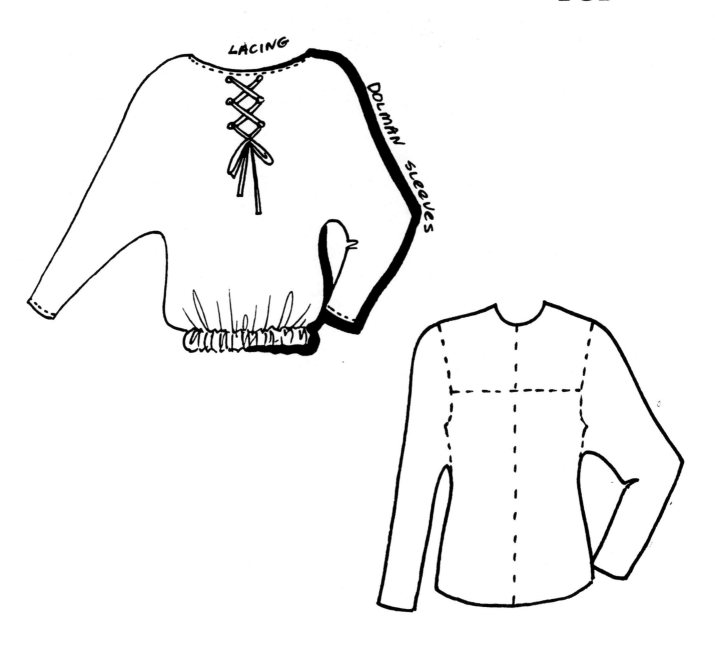

LACING

DOLMAN SLEEVES

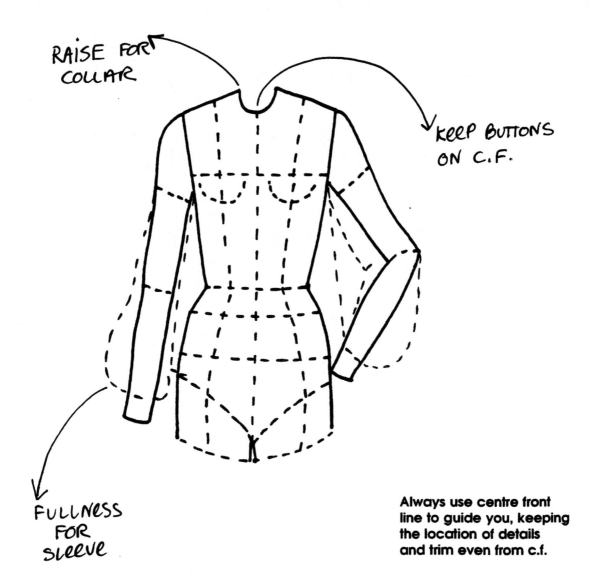

RAISE FOR COLLAR

KEEP BUTTONS ON C.F.

FULLNESS FOR SLEEVE

Always use centre front line to guide you, keeping the location of details and trim even from c.f.

BLOUSE

POINTED COLLAR

YOKE FRONT

CONVERTIBLE COLLAR

DROP SLEEVE

TIE FRONT

SHIRT

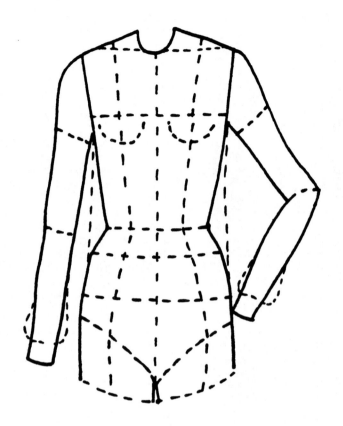

Continue to develop the
design on the croquis.
Use different hemlines,
pocket treatments, seam-
lines.

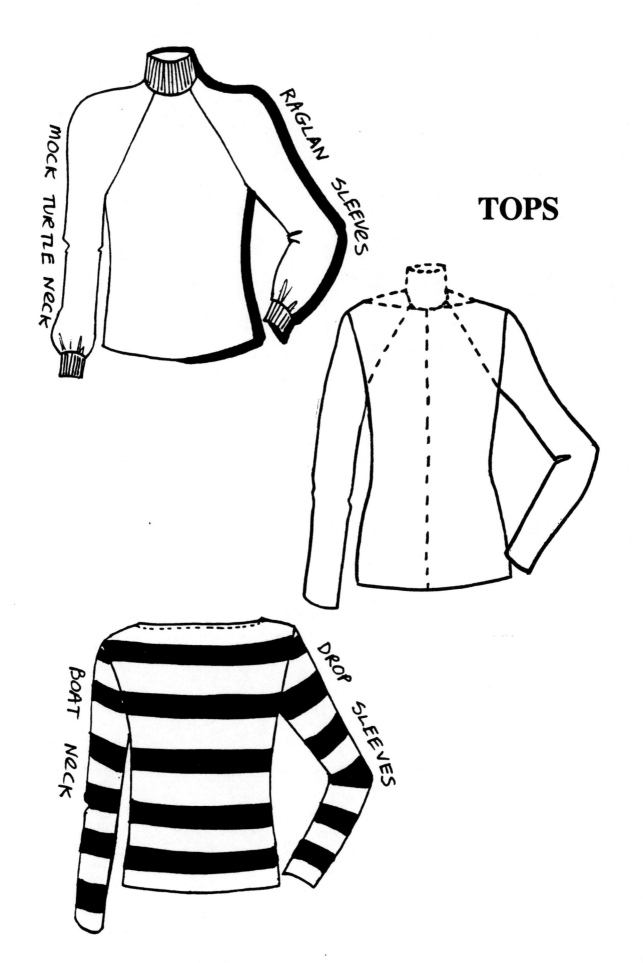

MOCK TURTLE NECK

RAGLAN SLEEVES

TOPS

BOAT NECK

DROP SLEEVES

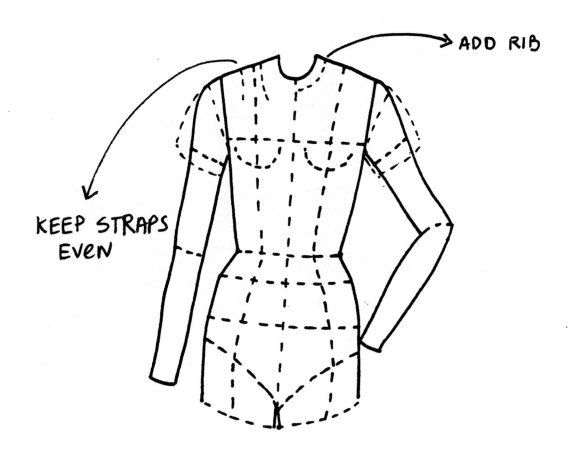

ADD RIB

KEEP STRAPS
EVEN

After tracing, draw
a new style using the same
silhouette.

TOPS

TOP STITCHING

TANK TOP

RIB NECKLINE

T-SHIRT

T-SHIRT

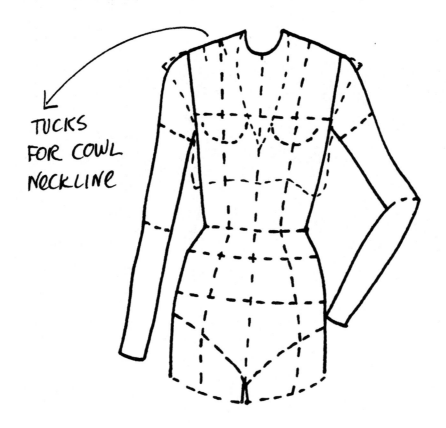

TUCKS
FOR COWL
NECKLINE

Practice different versions of these garments.

Repeat this process for the following tops.

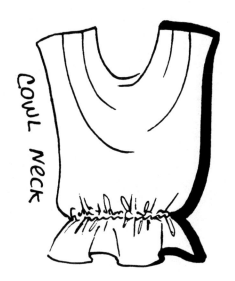

COWL NECK

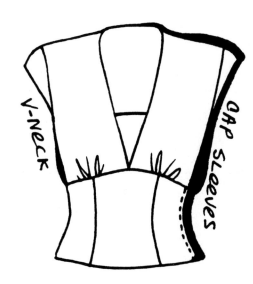

V-NECK

CAP SLEEVES

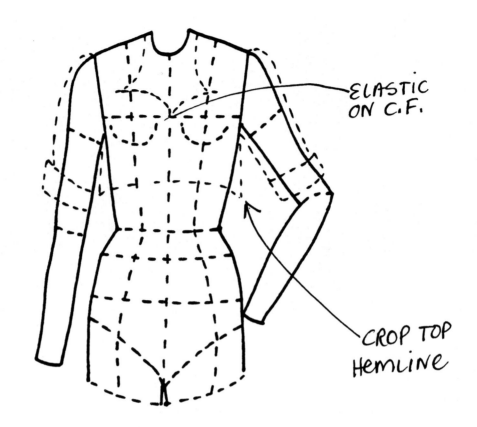

ELASTIC
ON C.F.

CROP TOP
HEMLINE

Try different sleeves and details.

TOPS

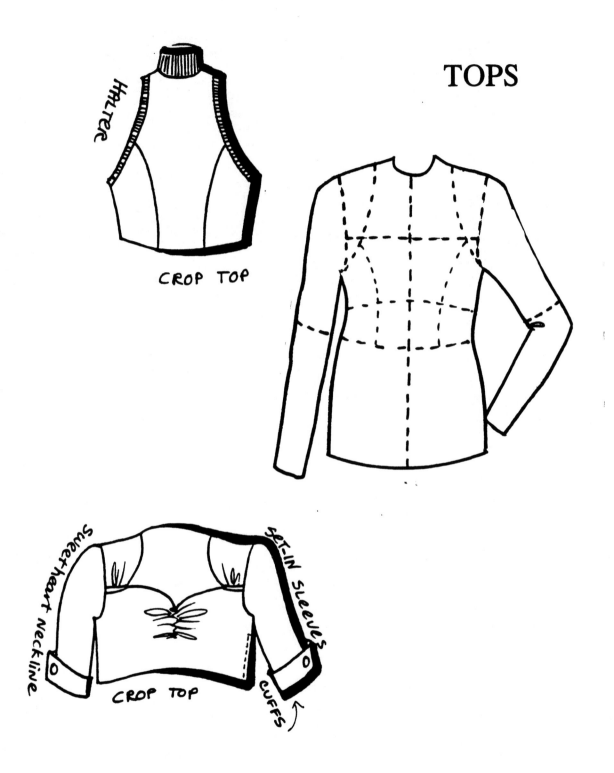

HALTER

CROP TOP

Sweetheart neckline

SET-IN SLEEVES

CROP TOP

CUFFS

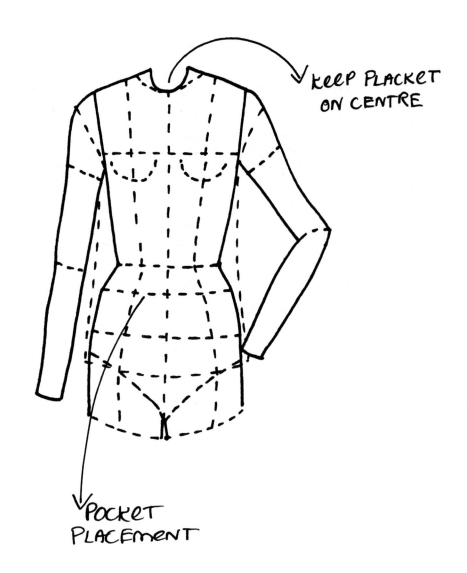

keep PLACKET
ON CENTRE

pocket
PLACEMENT

Try different necklines or collars.

54

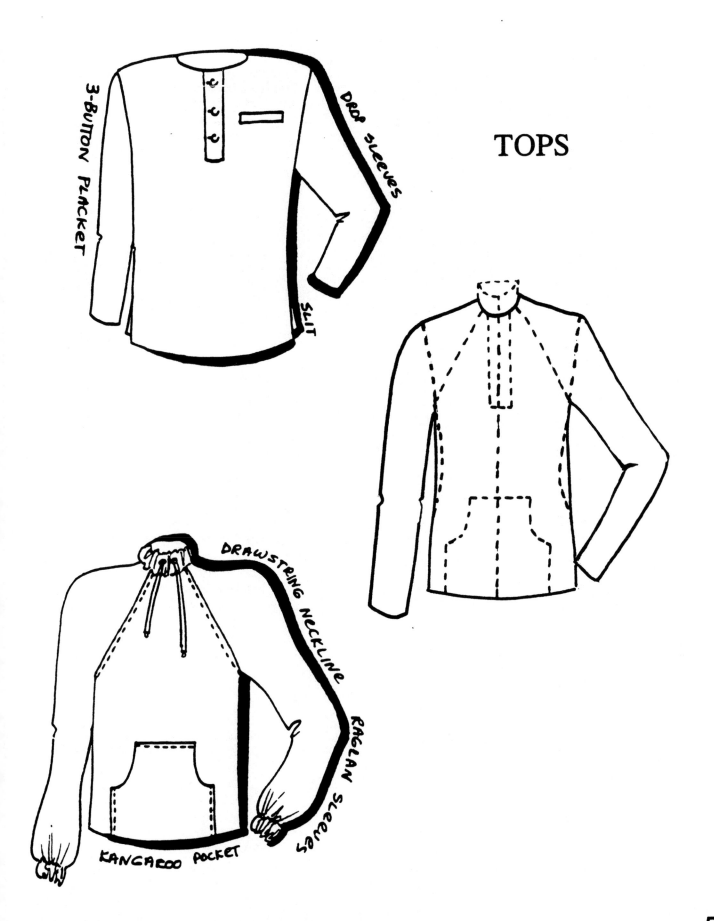

3-BUTTON PLACKET

DROP SLEEVES

SLIT

TOPS

DRAWSTRING NECKLINE

RAGLAN SLEEVES

KANGAROO POCKET

55

NOTCHED COLLAR

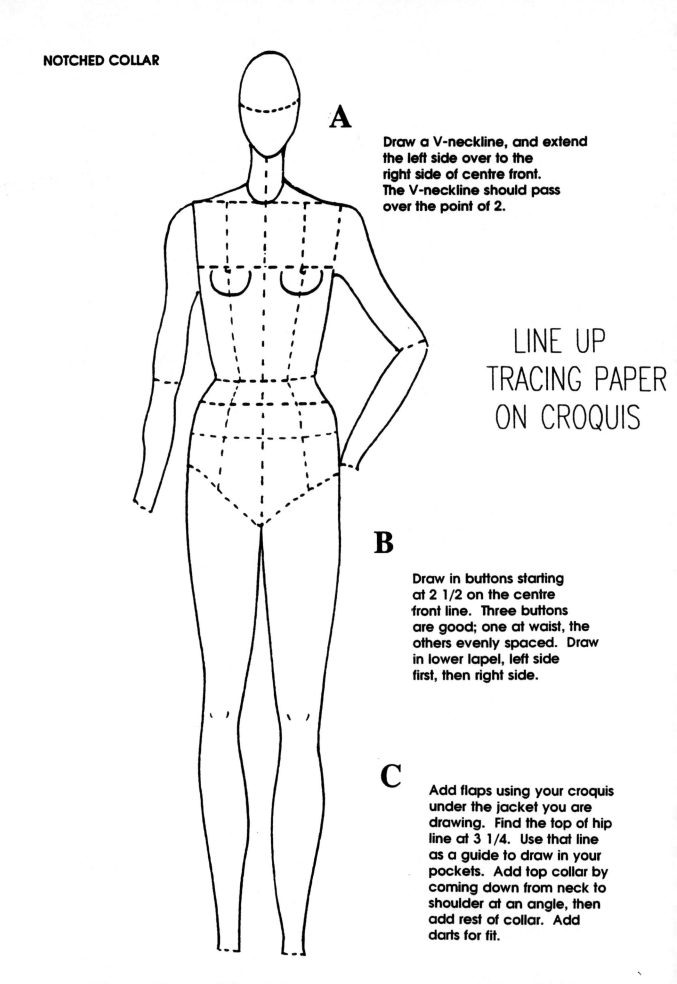

A

Draw a V-neckline, and extend the left side over to the right side of centre front. The V-neckline should pass over the point of 2.

LINE UP
TRACING PAPER
ON CROQUIS

B

Draw in buttons starting at 2 1/2 on the centre front line. Three buttons are good; one at waist, the others evenly spaced. Draw in lower lapel, left side first, then right side.

C

Add flaps using your croquis under the jacket you are drawing. Find the top of hip line at 3 1/4. Use that line as a guide to draw in your pockets. Add top collar by coming down from neck to shoulder at an angle, then add rest of collar. Add darts for fit.

TRY THIS AT LEAST FIVE TIMES BEFORE DOING A FINISHED FLAT. PRACTICE, PRACTICE!

1.

SIMPLE STEPS

2.

3.

FOR DRAWING

A NOTCHED

COLLAR JACKET

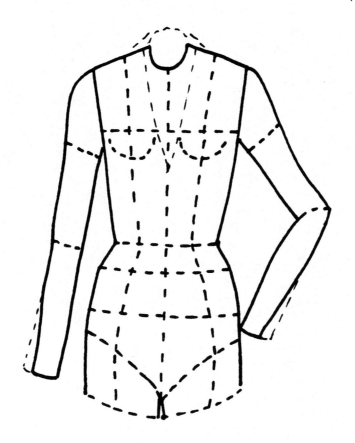

Carefully measure garment.
Note distance from centre
front to darts, tucks,
side seams. Keep them
equal in placement on
croquis.

SINGLE

BREASTED JACKET

SET-IN SLEEVES / STITCHED DARTS

NOTCHED COLLAR

PATCH POCKETS

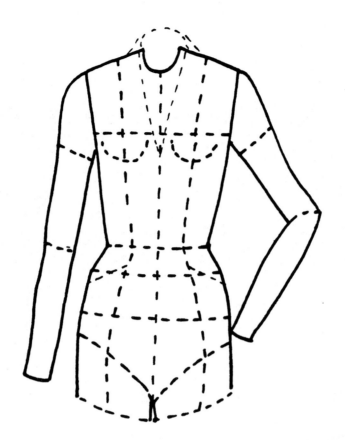

Continue to develop the
design on the croquis.
Use different hemlines,
pocket treatments, seam-
lines.

DOUBLE

BREASTED JACKET

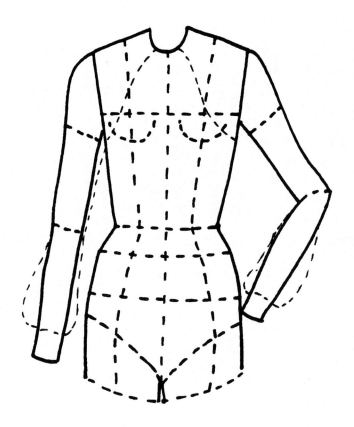

Draw a new style jacket
using the same silhouette.
Try different necklines
or collars. Try different
sleeves and details.

BASEBALL JACKET

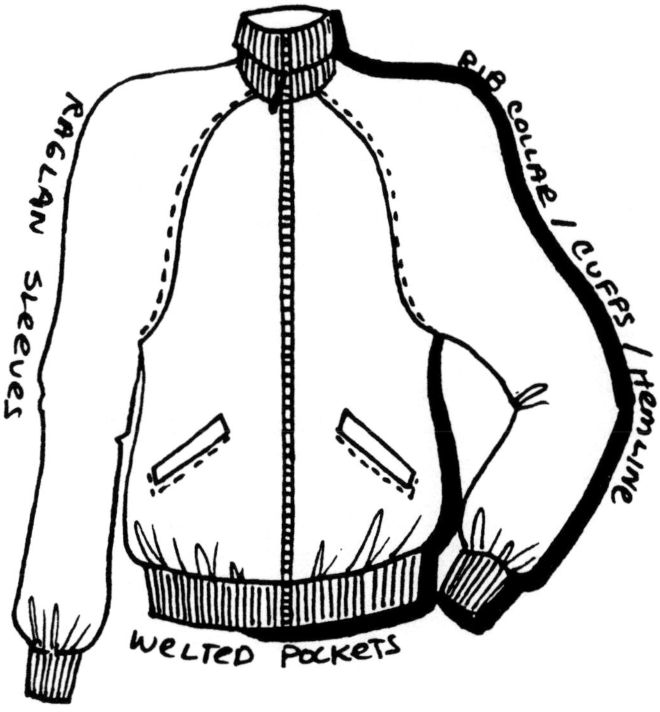

RAGLAN SLEEVES

RIB COLLAR / CUFFS / HEMLINE

WELTED POCKETS

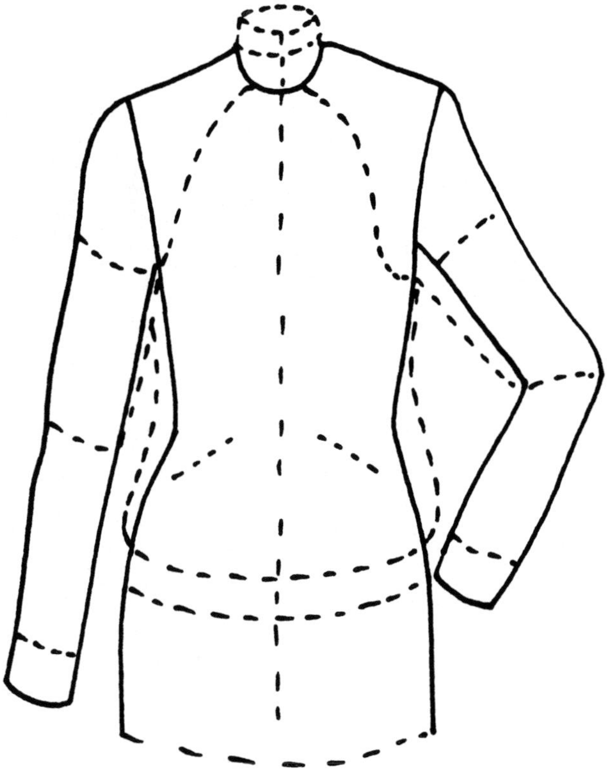

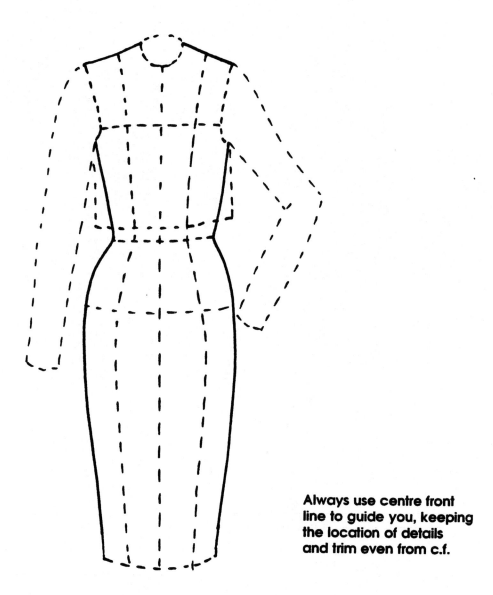

Always use centre front
line to guide you, keeping
the location of details
and trim even from c.f.

JACKETS

SET-IN SLEEVE

WING COLLAR

MIDRIFF LENGTH

STAND-UP COLLAR

RAGLAN SLEEVES

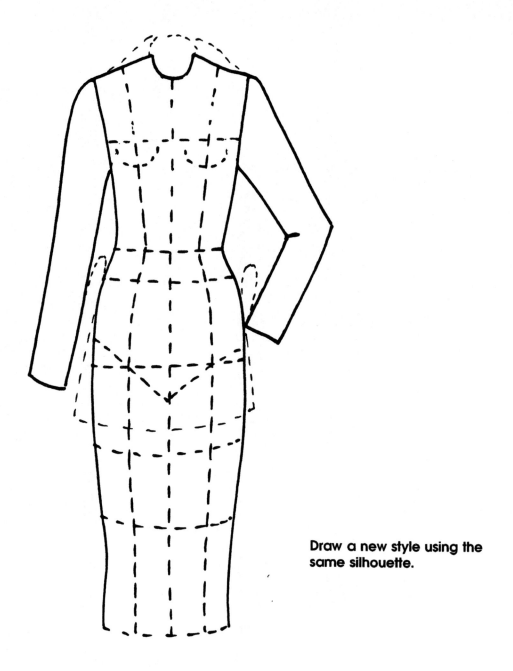

Draw a new style using the
same silhouette.

JACKET

SHAWL COLLAR

DOLMAN SLEEVE

TRIMMED COLLAR + CUFFS

**Practice drawing
versions of this garment.**

WRAP COAT

EPAULET

DROP SLEEVES

TIE BELT

Try different necklines or collars.

Try different sleeves and details.

DOUBLE BREASTED

COAT

SHAWL COLLAR

DOUBLE BREASTED COAT

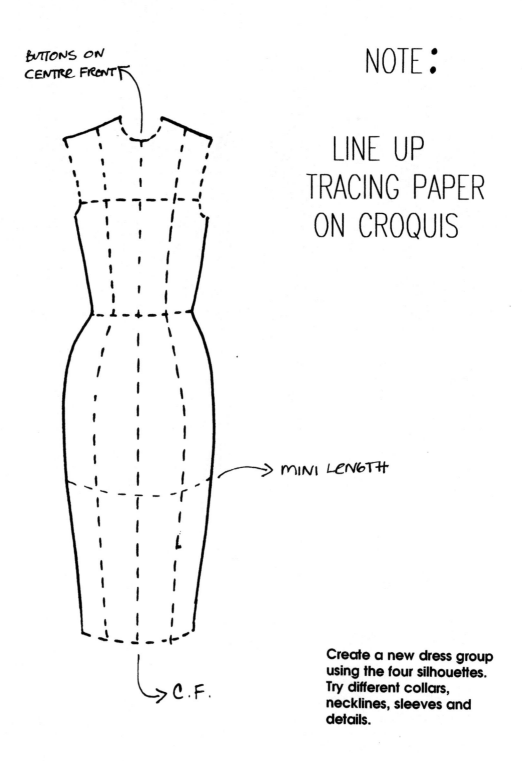

BUTTONS ON
CENTRE FRONT

NOTE:

LINE UP
TRACING PAPER
ON CROQUIS

MINI LENGTH

C.F.

Create a new dress group using the four silhouettes. Try different collars, necklines, sleeves and details.

72

DRESS GROUP

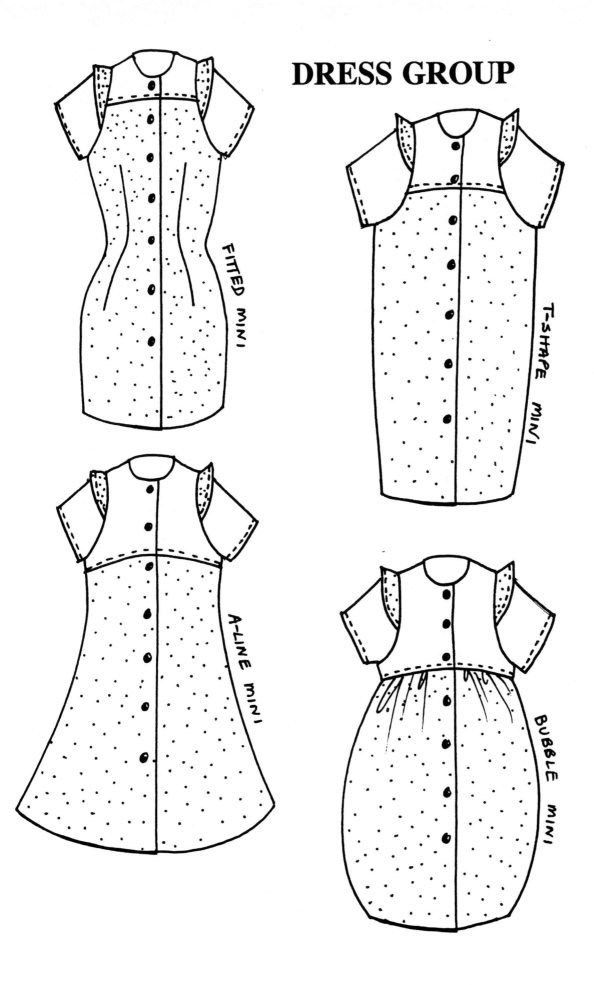

FITTED MINI

T-SHAPE MINI

A-LINE MINI

BUBBLE MINI

FITTED

DRESS GROUP

A-LINE

FITTED

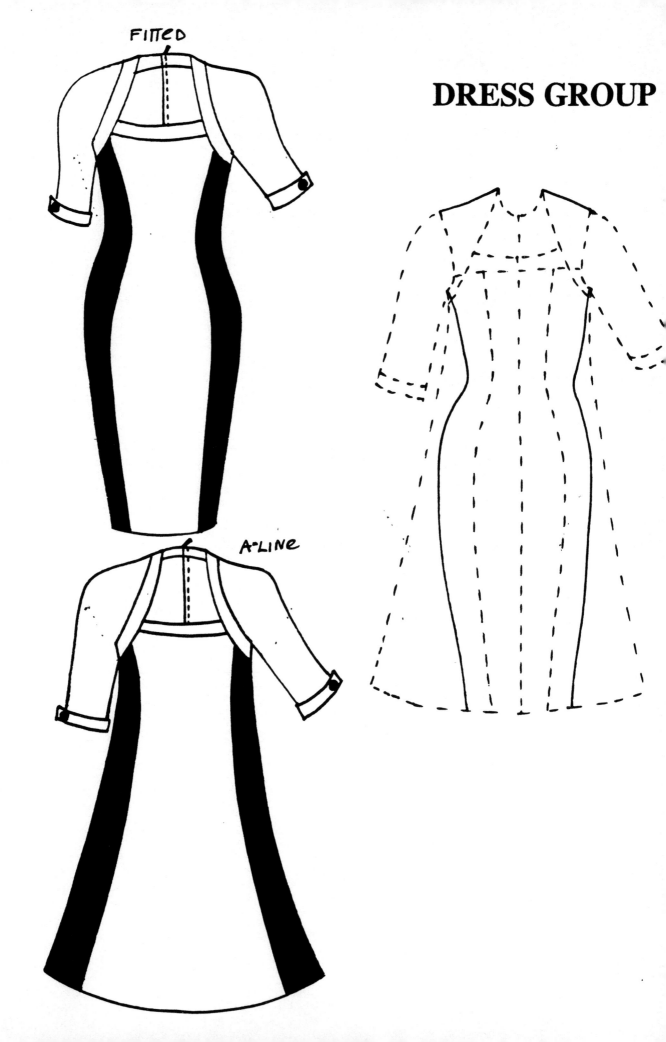

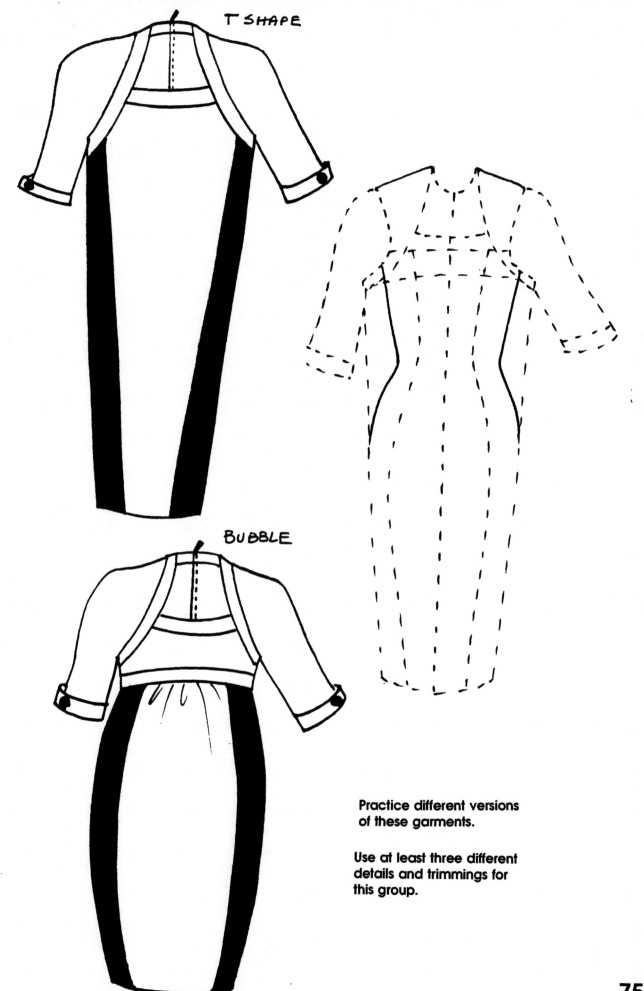

T SHAPE

BUBBLE

**Practice different versions
of these garments.**

**Use at least three different
details and trimmings for
this group.**

75

Create a five-piece group
using same details for all
pieces. Always use croquis
for equal measurement from
centre front.

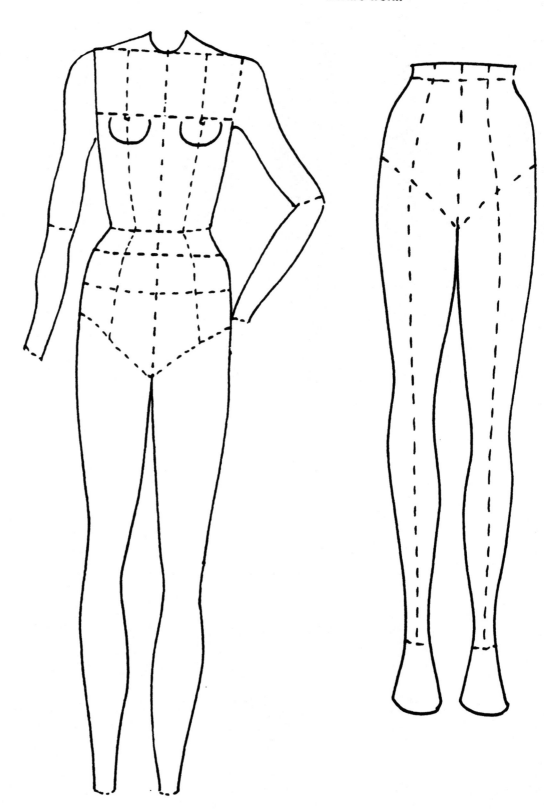

76

1. Top with gathered sleeve, ruffle hem.

2. Gathered skirt with peplum, lace hem.

3. Top with tie, ruffle collar.

4. Shorts with elastic waist, ruffle hem.

5. Knee length pant with elastic waist, lace and tie.

RUFFLE LACE GROUP

77